11802·2

Mark
with love from
Grandpa J.
Christmas 1991

Great Western
Steam in the
West Country

As storm clouds gather, No. 6024 *King Edward I* hurries across Worle Moor, on the approach to Weston-super-Mare, with the 5pm Paddington–Plymouth express. Despite the late hour (8pm) and the darkening sky, the country was still enjoying 'Double British Summer Time', thus making it possible for Norman Lockett to obtain this striking study of a locomotive which, happily, is again "alive and well". No. 6024, having been rescued from Barry scrapyard, has been restored to superb running order by the 6024 Preservation Society Ltd, at Quainton Road, Bucks, and is now based at Didcot.

9th June 1947

The Sunday working of the "Torbay Express" sweeps under Shaldon Bridge, west of Teignmouth, behind No. 7030 *Cranbrook Castle*. The fireman is able to enjoy the delights of the scenic Teign Estuary although, perhaps, he is resigned to a late arrival at Torquay. Norman Lockett, who made it his practice to record the exact time of each photograph, noted No. 7030 passing Shaldon Bridge at 4pm, only seven minutes before the booked arrival time at Torquay!

26th August 1956

THE NORMAN LOCKETT COLLECTION

Great Western
Steam in the
West Country

Mike Arlett & David Lockett

Oxford Publishing Co.

Near Cornwood – the scene of several of Norman Lockett's earliest photographs. The 12.30pm (Sundays) Penzance to Wolverhampton express climbs from Cornwood towards Ivybridge behind 'Castle' class, No. 5044 *Earl of Dunraven*.

3.55pm 21st August 1938

A FOULIS-OPC Railway Book

British Library Cataloguing in Publication Data
Great Western Steam in the West Country.
1. England. Railway services : Great Western Railway.
Steam locomotives, history
I. Arlett, Mike II. Lockett, David
625.2610942

ISBN 0-86093-480-2

Library of Congress catalog card number
90-84255

Published by:
Haynes Publishing Group
Sparkford, Near Yeovil, Somerset. BA22 7JJ

Haynes Publications Inc.
861 Lawrence Drive, Newbury Park, California 91320, USA.

Printed by: J.H. Haynes & Co. Ltd

Introduction

I became aware of the name Norman Lockett during my many years of friendship with Ivo Peters. Ivo had first met Norman when, by chance on 30th May 1956, both had decided to visit Bath Spa station to photograph the same train; the 5pm from Swindon to Bristol Temple Meads. This service was a regular 'running-in' turn for locomotives following overhaul at Swindon Works, thereby offering the opportunity to photograph an ex-GWR locomotive in 'ex-works' condition.

From this chance meeting, a lasting friendship developed, with numerous joint visits to photograph the railway scene throughout the British Isles.

Despite my best endeavours, my frequent visits to Ivo's home in Bath never coincided with those of Norman Lockett so, sadly, when he died in 1984, I had neither met him nor seen more than the handful of pictures which he had submitted for publication in the various railway periodicals. Ivo, who always sought and worked to the highest standards, often spoke of his late friend's photographs in the most enthusiastic terms, and on more than one occasion urged that I should try to see the collection for myself. Eventually I did so, but not without some difficulty in tracking down the whereabouts of Norman's son, David. Ironically, I found him living in Teignmouth, not a mile from where I and my family have spent an annual holiday for more years than I care to recall!

Despite the fact that I called all but unannounced, David and his wife welcomed me into their home and, during that first visit, were only too pleased to show me a selection from the photographic collection. This, together with other railway memorabilia, appeared to take up the greater part of their garage! I soon saw for myself that Ivo's appreciation of Norman Lockett's skills as a photographer was more than justified, and I was delighted to learn that David was giving thought to the publication of a book featuring some of his father's work. We later agreed that, to this end, I would assist in the selection of photographs and the preparation of accompanying captions.

A move to a new home early in 1989 enabled David to commence the unenviable task of creating a computer-based index of the negatives, most of which are glass-plates with the earliest dating back to 1934. In addition, there are 4,000 or so colour transparencies (to which must be added over 6,000 further negatives featuring Norman Lockett's other interests, which appear to have ranged from steam traction engines to church towers!).

In preparing this first volume of *The Norman Lockett Collection* we have sifted through several thousand prints and glass-plates. Every time I revisited David, yet more pictures had been 'discovered', so much so that reducing the material available to a choice of just 200 or so photographs for inclusion in this book, whilst a most enjoyable task, proved somewhat difficult!

In researching the history of many of the locomotives which appear within the following pages, I have made use of, and acknowledge the wealth of information contained in various books written by that champion of Great Western chroniclers, Mr O.S. Nock. In particular, the classic two-part history, *The GWR Stars, Castles & Kings* (published by David & Charles), has yielded much useful detail. Although we have used many of the

Norman Lockett A picture, at a lineside location far removed from the West Country, taken by Norman's great friend, Ivo Peters.

original enlargements produced by Norman himself, I also wish to thank Peter Skelton, who has taken considerable trouble to obtain prints from the original glass plate negatives. Some of these have, over the years, suffered from the ravages of time but which, because of their interest, are well worthy of inclusion.

To be associated with the publication of *The Norman Lockett Collection* is not only an exciting privilege, but a pleasure made possible by the kindness shown to me by David and Daphne Lockett. My thanks are also due to my wife, Sandra, who has yet to come to terms with arriving home to discover the lounge carpet yet again obliterated by dozens of large photographs. She has, however, assumed her customary role of 'having the last say' whenever the wide choice of photographs has left me undecided as to which should be selected!

Finally, on behalf of David and myself, thanks are due to our Publisher for allowing us to undertake all our own picture arrangements and layouts.

M.J. Arlett
North Bradley, Wilts

Norman Lockett and his Railway Photographic Collection –

some biographical details by David Lockett

I have always wanted a book of some of my father's 'Railway Photographic Collection' to be published. Over fifty of his pictures have been seen already in the books of other authors, but this is the first title featuring his material only.

The book has now come about via R. C. Riley's encouragement, the desire of his great friend, the late Ivo Peters, to have some of Norman's photographs included in the BBC book *The Train Now Departing* and the willing help of Mike Arlett. Mike and I have selected the pictures and agreed a journey order, with Mike writing all the captions. Such is the wealth of material available that deciding what to omit has caused us quite a headache. Assuming this album is well-received, we shall be producing further books from this collection in the years to come.

My greatest personal interest, previously, in 'railway' matters, was in the immediate post-war years, 1946-1950. Norman, my father, had been able to return to live at home in Weston-super-Mare after spending the war years being 'directed' to manage various branches of Boots the Chemist around the country. Weekend and Christmas visits had seemed to have been very brief previously, so my elder brother Geoffrey, and I enjoyed new ventures with our father. We accompanied him regularly on photographic expeditions to locations on the Weston loop line and the nearby Bristol-Taunton main line. As a matter of course we started to collect the engine numbers, and it was not long before Geoff and I arranged our own visits to Worle Junction for that purpose. We enjoyed and maintained a high degree of interest for the next five years, after which other matters and different priorities concerned us.

For Norman, railway photography was always a hobby. Yet, to this hobby he brought the very highest of standards. For me, it is the consistency of his high standards of picture composition, developing, enlarging and mounting, which makes his Collection so worthy of attention today. As a pharmacist he had been trained to think clearly, carefully and precisely, for the result of errors in his profession could have been fatal! Similarly, he thought much about his hobby, so that few photographs would fail to reach his own demanding standards. We now know that this was the general approach of most of the railway photographers of that era. They would consider many a picture of no consequence because of a small detail not being up to standard. Nowadays, such a photograph, despite any shortcomings, might well be of great historic interest or of general social value.

Another characteristic of my father, in relation to this hobby, was his singleness of mind. For him, railway

A Churchward 2-8-0, converted to oil-burning and renumbered 4855 (previously No. 3813), trundles down the main line near Weston-super-Mare with a heavy westbound freight. A photograph which dates from around the time when the post-war government-inspired programme to convert many locomotives to oil-burning, which included 20 of the GWR Churchward 2-8-0s, was abandoned.

6th March 1948

midsummer morn!

N. Lockett 1955

A folio print (here reduced in size), typical of the work submitted by Normal Lockett to the Railway Photographic Society. Mogul No. 5376 heads a mid-morning freight along the sea wall between Teignmouth and Parson's Tunnel.

photography was a very personal hobby from which little distracted him during his lifetime. His records of each photograph are very extensive and include the following details. The consecutive number and details of the train and location, the engine wheel arrangement, number and name (if applicable), the date and time. Also recorded were the photographic details: lens aperture stop number (f number), the shutter speed and a brief comment on the light, the type of plate used and the development details. Consequently, we have records of many trackside scenes covering the years from 1934 to 1983. To be precise, 1st April 1934 to 6th October 1983, that is, apart from the war years, during which time he took no 'shots' of trains. Personally, I find these notes quite staggering:

Thornton-Pickard Reflex Camera (Glass Plate) – Quarter Plate Size.

No. 528 15.8.1939 near Trerule Signal Box.

No. 529 12.6.1946 near Brean Road.

Perfect sequence, with a gap of nearly seven years! No fuss, no explanation – perhaps a reflection of the British 'Bulldog' spirit. Hitler's war was a mere inconvenience or interruption of seven years but the normal things of life just continue, without remark or comment!

For many years, on his photographic expeditions, my father used public transport only, both trains and buses. He carried quite a load – a case in each hand with a camera, a dozen slide-holders loaded with unexposed glass plates for each camera; notebooks, timetables, sandwiches and a raincoat. In fact, it was not until the time of his friendship with Ivo Peters, during the 1960s, that Norman used alternative transport. The two of them, with others from time to time, travelled the length and breadth of the country in Ivo's Bentley, photographing trains in the sunset years of steam power. Consequently, Dad's pre-1960 locations reflect his ability to travel to them from home. Between 1933 and 1940 he lived in Plymouth, to which city he had moved from his home town of Weston-super-Mare. His training as a pharmacist began in 1925 – four years as an apprentice with Boots the Chemists in that town, followed by four years as a student at the Merchant Venturers' College of Pharmacy in Bristol. He was registered as a chemist and druggist and became a member of the Pharmaceutical Society on the 5th April 1933. Thus, many of the pre-war photos are taken in the Plymouth area, at such places as Hemerdon Bank and Cornwood.

After the war, Norman was appointed manager of the Boots Southmead Branch, Bristol. He worked a twelve hour day (including travelling time from Weston-super-Mare), except for Wednesdays, when he had a half-day. Each Thursday and Saturday he worked an additional hour of rota-duty, when the shop remained open an extra hour from 6pm to 7pm for prescriptions, so he would arrive home at 8.30pm on those days. Photographs in the Weston-super-Mare area were taken mostly on Sundays and Wednesday afternoons and on some of those occasions he was accompanied by a child or two. Longer day excursions had always formed part of his programme and, additionally, he regularly spent his annual holidays in the Shap area of Westmorland. Easter, Whitsun and August Bank Holiday Mondays (the latter being the first Monday in the month in those days) were occasions of expeditions of greater distances. I remember well my brother Geoff, and I going to Honiton Bank in Devon and Wellington Bank in Somerset. En route to Wellington Bank one year, we children thought it a great achievement to be able to stand in two different counties at the same time! We stood with one foot in Somerset and the other in Devon at the boundary stone that was then on the main A38 road.

Trips to the South West were only possible if Norman did not have to open the shop for rota-duty on the Bank Holiday from 6-7pm. Invariably he had to, so we would spend those days at Mangotsfield or Yate, to enable us to return to the shop by the correct time. It was my youngest brother Philip, who travelled regularly with his father to the Teignmouth area in the fifties, when many shots were taken on the Sea Wall, at Parson's Tunnel and near Shaldon Bridge. It is ironic that in later years Teignmouth was to play such a major part in my own life. I moved there in 1965 in order to complete a three-year course at Moorlands Bible College, situated, at that time, in nearby Holcombe. I subsequently taught the Scriptures at Kirkstead College, Torquay (1968-70) and at the Beacon School, Teignmouth (1971-87).

In April 1969, Norman relinquished his responsibility as manager of Boots Milsom Street Branch, Bath, in accordance with company policy, having completed twelve years service there. He, my mother Louise, sister Norma and brother Philip, had moved to live in Bath in November 1957. Norman continued to work for five days per week however, doing relief work in various other shops of the company. This was reduced to three days per week in 1974 until his final retirement on 31st March 1979, when my parents returned to live in Weston-super-Mare. Throughout the years, my father had remained faithful to his hobby and his Railway Photographic Collection had grown in size considerably. The actual "photographing" season would last roughly from

After calling at Weston-super-Mare, an immaculate 'Castle', No. 5097 *Sarum Castle,* heads a 12-coach Liverpool–Plymouth express around the long curved approach towards Uphill Junction, where the main line from Bristol to Taunton will be regained.

10th October 1952

The start of a long and happy friendship. No. 6009 *King Charles II* approaches Bath Spa on the evening running-in turn with the 5pm Swindon to Bristol local. This was the occasion of the chance meeting between Norman and Ivo Peters, both of whom had turned up at Bath Spa to photograph the same train.

30th May 1956

April to October each year. The developing of plates would be carried out late at night, usually within a week or so of the photographs being taken. Printing, enlarging and mounting would be effected in the 'closed' season – November to March. Incidentally, Dad was no mean gardener and somehow always managed to sow seeds and put plants in by the appropriate time. He also followed the fortunes of Somerset County Cricket Club with interest, although his physical support at matches was limited to a day or two at the Weston or Bath Festival.

From 1979, much of the Collection was housed with me in Teignmouth, whilst Norman concentrated on updating his records by "borrowing" from me the relevant portion. When he died, suddenly, from a stroke early in 1984, he had completed most of his notes for all colour slides taken up to 1983. Details are missing for the first colour slides only – those taken between 1958 and 1961, which appear to have been considered as "experimental" by my father.

Following a warning from my doctor, I retired as headmaster of the Beacon School on health grounds, at the end of the academic year in 1987. Twelve months or so later, after an unexpected visit from a stranger called Mike Arlett, the process began for the production of this book. I am very pleased that it contains some photographs from a booklet that I came across recently. This had been prepared by my father in about 1948, but never published, consisting of pre-Nationalisation shots. Although I now recall the existence of it I have to admit that I had forgotten completely about it. We trust that the calibre of the photography produced in this book will provide railway enthusiasts with a lasting memory of the greatness of Great Western trains.

Newton Abbot, 1990

Part 1: Bristol to the West Country

The first, and major part of this book, follows the original Great Western line to the West Country; the route of the old Bristol & Exeter line via Bridgwater and Taunton. Then onwards past Exeter to Torbay, Plymouth and into south east Cornwall.

It is only proper that our journey, featuring Great Western motive-power in the West Country, should commence at Bristol for Temple Meads station was the railway 'gateway' to the West. Even after 1906, when much of the through traffic between Paddington and Exeter was diverted via Westbury and Castle Cary, Bristol was to remain one of the most important and busy railway centres in Great Britain. Temple Meads was, of course, a joint station shared with the Midland Railway, but the Great Western was always the dominant partner.

Titled Trains at Bristol, Temple Meads

Above: The "Cornishman". 'Castle' class 4-6-0, No. 5045 *Earl of Dudley,* rolls into Temple Meads at 12.23pm with the 'down' "Cornishman"; the 9.15am Wolverhampton to Penzance service. The curved approach to the east end of the station provided a superb setting for the railway photographer especially, as here, on those occasions when the adjacent lines were free of traffic. No. 5045 is seen prior to the fitting of a double chimney.
3rd October 1953

Left: The "Bristolian". Always an exciting spectacle; the departure of the "Bristolian" from platform 9 at Temple Meads, sharp on 4.30pm. No. 7014 *Caerhays Castle,* about to set off on the 105 minutes dash to Paddington, had only recently returned from Swindon Works following an overhaul which included the fitting of a double chimney, a feature which many considered spoilt the classic lines of this famous GWR class but which, without doubt, added significantly to an already impressive performance.

20th April 1955

No. 6029 *King Edward VIII* coasts into platform 9 with an early evening relief train to Paddington. No. 6029, the last of the famous GWR 'King' class to be built at Swindon, entered service in August 1930 bearing the name *King Stephen,* but was renamed in May 1936.

3rd August 1959

Bristol Temple Meads: The Western End

During the post-war era of steam, Temple Meads station was a wonderful place for the railway enthusiast and photographer. There was always something going on, although this involved frequent 'excursions' from one end of the station to the other. After walking the full length of the station several times, you began to appreciate just how long some of those platforms were! However, as we intend to journey westward from Bristol, the content of these two pages concentrates on activities to be seen at the western end of Temple Meads.

Ivatt 2-6-2T No. 41208 pulls away from platform 1 with the 3.50pm service to Portishead. The train would run down the relief main line for two miles, before crossing on to the branch to Portishead at Parson's Street Junction.

19th September 1956

Mixed traffic class, No. 6860 *Aberporth Grange* ambles through the station with a parcels' train, passing BR Class 3 2-6-2T No. 82035. To the right side of the photograph can be seen Bristol Temple Meads Loco Yard box, which controlled all movements to and from Bath Road motive power depot.

27th April 1961

Another of the titled trains to call at Temple Meads – the "Merchant Venturer", the 4.35pm from Weston-super-Mare to Paddington, runs in behind No. 6900 *Abney Hall*. This train waited at Bristol for 15 minutes before setting off again, calling at Bath, Chippenham, Swindon and Reading, reaching Paddington at 8pm.

26th May 1958

Bristol, Bath Road Shed

Locospotters used the western end of platform 4 to view the comings and goings at Bath Road locomotive shed. How much better though, for Norman Lockett who, with the benefit of a lineside pass, could obtain close-up views of ex-GWR engines being prepared for their next turns of duty.

'On parade.' Awaiting their next duties, No. 7033 *Hartlebury Castle,* No. 6986 *Rydal Hall* and (right) No. 1009 *County of Carmarthen,* are lined up outside the running shed. 16th August 1959

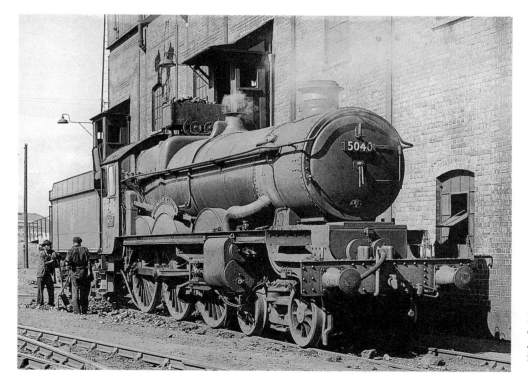

Earlier the same afternoon, Norman obtained this photograph of No. 5040 *Stokesay Castle* receiving attention at the coaling stage.

16th August 1959

A Railway Correspondence & Travel Society (RCTS) special train, hauled by No. 6841 *Marlas Grange* at Avonmouth Docks.
21st July 1963

Avonmouth Docks

The large and busy dock complex at Avonmouth was shunted by the Port of Bristol's own fleet of locomotives. Very appropriately, these were all built by two Bristol-based companies, Avonside and Peckett, and all were given the names associated with areas in and around the city.

For the tour around the dockside lines, the RCTS special was hauled by Peckett-built 0-6-0 saddle tank (No. 2036 of 1943) No. S11 *Bristol*. The 'S' prefix had been added to the numbers of all of the Port of Bristol's steam locomotives, following the introduction of diesel shunting engines.

21st July 1963

The 8am Plymouth to Liverpool speeds through the cutting on the approach to Flax Bourton Tunnel, hauled by No. 7029 *Clun Castle,* still in original condition. No. 7029 was destined to become the last of the 'Castles' to remain in service, and upon withdrawal in December 1965, was purchased privately for preservation.

7th June 1954

As befits a 'titled' train; No. 7014 *Caerhays Castle* appears in pristine condition, awaiting the 'right-away' with the 'up' "Bristolian".

Bristol Temple Meads

The problem with reporting numbers is you cannot see the smokebox numberplate! In the 1950s, Norman Lockett looked upon colour photography very much as 'second best' to the quality obtainable with black and white. "Not to be taken seriously" is the terse comment in one of his notebooks! As a result, Norman did not keep details and dates of many of his earlier colour transparencies.

This unidentified 'County' is seen approaching Temple Meads in May 1959 with the 9.10am Liverpool to Plymouth service.

With the blower just cracked open, No. 7014 *Caerhays Castle* is featured again, awaiting departure from platform 9 with the "Bristolian".

The impressive and evocative sight of a top-link locomotive; a 'Castle' restarts the 'up' "Merchant Venturer" away from Temple Meads, watched by the fireman of 2-6-2T, No. 5561, engaged on somewhat more humble duties.

Bristol Temple Meads

With steam to spare, 'Castle' class No. 5043 *Earl of Mount Edgcumbe* stands at platform 6 with stock bearing a mixture of both the original and later styles of BR liveries.

In early August 1959, No. 3803 runs through the station, on the middle road between platforms 2 and 4, with a train of empty coaching stock, passing a 'Castle'-hauled westbound express waiting at platform 4.

Empty Stock Workings

Fresh from overhaul, which included a repaint in green livery, GWR Mogul No. 6384 emerges from the gloom of the overall roof on one of the through lines between platforms 7 and 9 with a train of empty stock.

Preparing to leave for the West. The fireman of No. 7000 *Viscount Portal* is busy shovelling coal forward on a well-stocked tender.

Departure and Arrival

Mogul No. 7316 runs in from Weston-super-Mare with what appears to be the "Merchant Venturer" stock. Pity about those two leading coaches!

No. 4083 *Abbotsbury Castle* sets back towards the main running shed at Bath Road.

Bath Road Motive Power Depot

A general view of the motive power depot including, on the left, the large coaling stage surmounted by the water storage tanks. Good varieties of locomotives are on view.

Collett 0-4-2T No. 1410, pulls away from the 'up' bay platform at Yatton for the run along the single-line branch to Clevedon. The coach in the 'blood and custard' livery is standing in the 'down' bay platform which served as the starting point for trains over the Cheddar Valley line to Witham.

Yatton

No. 1463 heads out of Yatton, passing the large signal box. I wanted to include this photograph as it represents one of those rare occasions when Ivo Peters was 'captured' by Norman. (More usually, it was the other way around!)

In lined-green livery, 0-4-2T No. 1463 sets off to Clevedon, passing, on the left, the small shed which, until recently, had housed the branch line locomotive.

The Clevedon Branch

No. 1463 bowls along the branch with an afternoon train to Clevedon.

Yatton

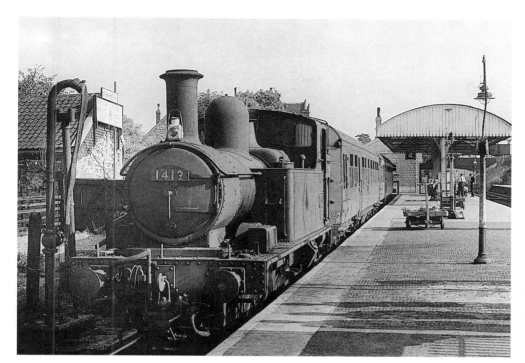

Yatton station, twelve miles west of Bristol Temple Meads, was the junction for two branch lines; the Cheddar Valley line which turned southwards to Witham, near Frome, and the $3\frac{1}{2}$ mile line to Clevedon. In the latter years of steam, the single-line Clevedon branch was operated by ex-GWR Collett motor fitted 0-4-2Ts.

No. 1412 simmers away in the 'up' platform bay at Yatton, waiting for custom from a main line connecting service. Seen to the left is an elderly water column, complete with a 'fire devil' which was fired up during periods of very cold weather to prevent the water supply in the column from freezing.
2nd October 1959

No. 1463, in lined-green livery and well-polished, starts the Sundays only 5.40pm service out of Yatton on the final day of steam-hauled passenger operation over the branch. On the following day, the Yatton–Clevedon service was 'dieselized', but the branch line survived only a further six years.

7th August 1960

Yatton and the Clevedon Branch

No. 1412 pulls away from Yatton with the mid-afternoon auto-working to Clevedon.
2nd October 1959

No. 1454, with an elderly ex-GWR auto-coach in tow, heads down the branch with the 6.37pm Yatton–Clevedon service.
17th August 1955

No. 1412 is seen again, this time setting off down the branch with the 4.19pm service to Clevedon.

2nd October 1959

The Cheddar Valley Line

Two photographs, taken near Axbridge some two miles north-west of Cheddar, showing a class 4575 2-6-2T, No. 5554, with the 7pm Wells to Yatton train, and Collett 0-6-0 No. 2215, with a Wells to Bristol branch freight. One of the many strawberry beds which bordered the branch, and once provided much seasonal traffic, can be seen to the right of the trackbed.

4th July 1951

No. 4088 *Dartmouth Castle* has turned off the main line at Worle Junction, and heads the 4.15pm Paddington to Plymouth along the loop line serving Weston-Super-Mare. The signal box controlling the junction at Worle can be seen behind the rear of the train. The original main line, by-passing Weston, runs behind the hedgerow seen to the right of the picture.

10th June 1953

Crossing now to the original main line, 2-8-2T No. 7250, heads east towards Bristol with a heavy class C freight.
19th July 1953

Near Worle Junction

When the Bristol & Exeter Railway was opened to public traffic, between Bristol and Bridgwater, on 14th June 1841, the route of the line ran some way to the south-east of the then small seaside resort of Weston-super-Mare. This was in deference to local opponents, and the town was, instead, linked to the main line by a $1\frac{1}{2}$ mile branch, originally worked by 'horse-power'. As the popularity of Weston grew throughout the 1840s, opinions changed, and proposals to construct a loop-line, were welcomed by residents and visitors alike. The loop-line opened in the 1850s and was nearly four miles in length. It extended from Worle Junction to the east, rejoining the main line at Uphill Junction to the south of Weston.

Ministry of Supply 'Austerity' 2-8-0 No. 77380 trundles down the main line towards Uphill Junction, with a westbound class H freight.

9th June 1947

Looking westwards, No. 4985 *Allesley Hall* approaches Worle Junction with an excursion from Taunton to Treherbert. Weston Milton Halt, built on the eastern outskirts of the town, lay immediately beyond the overbridge in the background.

19th September 1954

Locking Road Arrivals and Departures

Above left: During the 1950s, the impressive Churchward 4700 class 2-8-0 mixed traffic locomotives could be seen, particularly during the peak summer season, on express passenger duties. No. 4703, looking as if she is fresh from overhaul, eases an excursion over the points leading into Locking Road station.

12th August 1956

Above: An excursion from Birmingham runs in behind ex-LMS Stanier Class 5 4-6-0, No. 45150.

25th May 1958

Left: No. 5965 *Woollas Hall* draws a train of empty coaching stock out from Locking Road. A 2-6-2T stands adjacent to the water tower, whilst another 'Hall' waits to run onto the turntable.

31st July 1955

The 12.15pm (SO) Weston–Sheffield pulls out of Locking Road station, and snakes over the crossings behind LMS 'Crab' 5MT class 2-6-0 No. 42827. Other locomotives wait with their trains in the carriage sidings on the extreme left.

26th June 1954

Weston-super-Mare

The arrival of the railway was to have an enormous effect on Weston which, being the nearest West Country seaside resort linked by rail to Birmingham and the Midlands, gained rapidly in popularity. Such was the growth in traffic that a special 'excursion' station, comprising four platforms, was built. This new station, which became known as Locking Road, lay adjacent and to the north of the existing General station. The lines serving both stations joined at a point where the railway was crossed by a road bridge, and this became a favourite location for Norman Lockett, which is featured both here, and in one of the colour sections of this book.

Sunday Departures from Weston

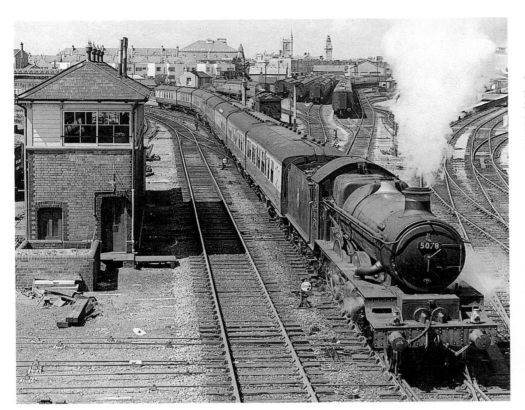

'Castle' class, No. 5078 *Beaufort,* pulls away from Weston-super-Mare General with the 8.45am (Sundays) Plymouth to Liverpool, passing the signal box controlling the junction with the lines leading into Locking Road.

15th May 1955

The same Sundays-only service is featured again, but in 1953 the train conveyed through carriages to Manchester, in addition to Liverpool. No. 7029 *Clun Castle* heads past the signal box, but note the changed position of the point rodding. This, and the altered position of the flue-pipes projecting through the roof, suggests that the lever frame in the box may have been renewed and resited between 1953 and 1955.

17th May 1953

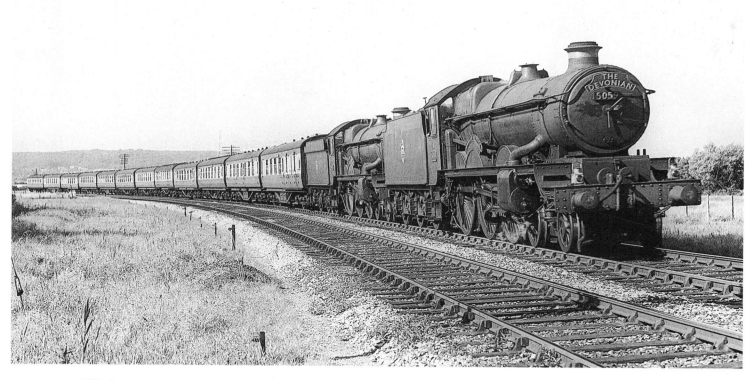

'Westbound Devonian'. Having called at Weston-super-Mare, the westbound "Devonian" runs towards Uphill Junction behind a pair of 'Castle' class 4-6-0s, No. 5059 *Earl St Aldwyn* piloting No. 5041 *Tiverton Castle.*
4th August 1953

Between Weston and Uphill

Leaving Weston-super-Mare General station, the line turns southwards towards the junction with the original main line at Uphill.

'An elderly lady with 13 on!' 'Star' class 4-6-0, No. 4056 *Princess Margaret,* built in 1914 and seen here with the elbow-pattern steam pipes fitted in 1949, runs towards Weston with the heavily-laden 11.20am (Sundays) Plymouth to Wolverhampton. No. 4056 was withdrawn from traffic in October 1957, the last of this once-famous GWR class to remain in service.

5th July 1953

Originally built for the Ministry of Munitions, a hundred of these 2-8-0s were taken over by the Great Western after the First World War. Although re-equipped with many GWR fittings, they always retained their original Great Central Railway type boilers. No. 3024 heads a long rake of mineral wagons down the main line.

22nd July 1947

Near Uphill Junction

The number 111 was carried originally by the GWR's only 4-6-2 Pacific – *The Great Bear*. In 1924, when the 'Bear' required heavy repairs, the decision was taken to rebuild the locomotive as a 'Castle' class 4-6-0, the latter class having been introduced the previous autumn. Retaining the number 111, the rebuilt locomotive was renamed *Viscount Churchill*. It is seen here heading away from Uphill Junction towards Weston, with the 1.15pm Plymouth to Paddington.

13th April 1952

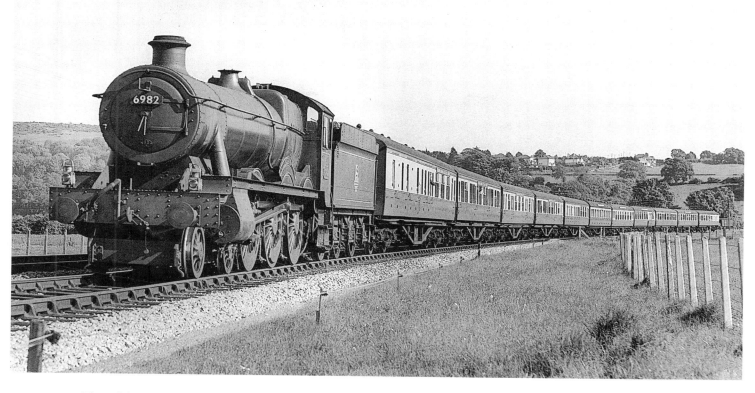

The origins of the GWR 'Hall' class go back to 1925 and the rebuilding of a former 'Saint' class, No. 2925, which, fitted with 6ft driving wheels and other improvements, became the prototype 'Hall', No. 4900 *Saint Martin.* From 1928, the GWR built no less than 259 of these useful locomotives, and commencing in 1944, a further series of 71 'Modified Halls' were constructed which incorporated one-piece plate frames. One of this latter type, No. 6982 *Melmerby Hall,* runs towards Weston with the 11.20am (Sundays) Plymouth to Wolverhampton.

24th May 1953

On the main line between the junctions at Worle and Uphill, 2-8-0 No. 2808, passes with a class H freight bound for Taunton and the West.

9th October 1948

Uphill Junction

'Modified Hall', No. 6997 *Bryn-Ivor Hall*, rejoins the main line, passing Uphill Junction signal box with a Bristol to Taunton train.

September 1957

Churchward Mogul No. 6372 swings away from the main line with the 4.30pm Taunton to Paddington. The Mogul, seen with lined-green livery, would be removed from this train at Bristol, having called at all stations between Taunton and Weston. Thereafter the train served only principal stations to Paddington.

23rd May 1956

Uphill Cutting

Just beyond Uphill Junction, the main line passes through a deep cutting, towards the south end of which the road from Uphill to Bleadon is carried high above the rails on a graceful single-span bridge.

Above: No. 4940 *Ludford Hall,* one of the original series introduced in 1928, heads westwards from Uphill Junction with a 'down' parcels train. The signal box can just be seen on the 'up' side of the line beyond the bridge.

13th May 1956

Right: No. 1012 *County of Denbigh* passes through the attractive tree-lined cutting with the 1.05pm (Sundays) Plymouth to Paddington express. Still fitted with the original design of single chimney, No. 1012 and the other 'Counties' were instantly recognisable at a distance by the flat-topped wheel splashers, a straight nameplate and the pronounced taper to the boiler.

22nd May 1955

With an interesting variety of coaching stock in tow, 'Bulldog' class 4-4-0, No. 3363 *Alfred Baldwin,* passes Brean Road Halt with the 5.15pm semi-fast service from Bristol to Taunton. Until closure in May 1955, the isolated halt at Brean Road (some three miles south of Weston), served Brean Sands and the nearby village of Lympsham.

15th June 1937

Bleadon Level

From Bleadon & Uphill station, the railway ran due south across the exposed and windswept Bleadon Level.

In the early evening, a Churchward-designed Mogul, No. 6301, sweeps along the levels near Brean Road with a train of empty coaching stock.

19th June 1946

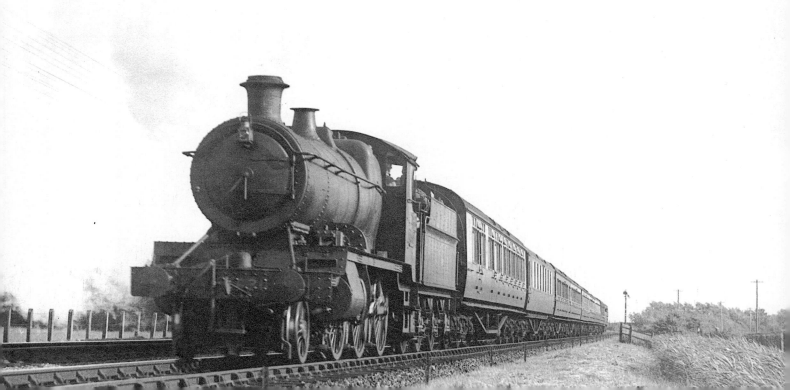

At the same location as the previous photograph, and some 15 minutes later, No. 6014 *King Henry VII* speeds towards Bristol with the "North Mail". No. 6014 had been partially 'streamlined' in 1935, and although only a short-lived experiment, evidence is still visible here with the splayed front to the locomotive cab.

19th June 1946

A near gale force wind, blowing off the Severn Estuary, snatches the exhaust from a grimy Collett 2-8-0, No. 3833, as it battles down the main line with a heavy freight bound for Taunton.

9th July 1947

One of the best-loved class of Great Western locomotives – a 'Saint' 4-6-0, No. 2981 *Ivanhoe,* races across the Levels at 60mph with a North to West express.

23rd June 1937

Near Brean Road

'Rebirth of a hobby.' After a wartime break of nearly seven years, Norman Lockett was at last able to recommence his love of railway photography. This, Norman's very first post-war 'shot', shows 2-8-0 No. 2828 trundling southwards with a westbound freight.

12th June 1946

Last Day at Tucker Street

The first colour section in this book featured the line to Clevedon, while the other branch from Yatton, the Cheddar Valley line, is shown here, albeit on a sad occasion.

On the final day of passenger traffic over the Yatton–Witham branch, Ivatt 2-6-2T No. 41245 is seen after arrival with the 1.45pm (SO) from Yatton, which terminated at Wells, Tucker Street to form a return working to Yatton.

7th September 1963

Weston-super-Mare

No. 4098 *Kidwelly Castle* sets off from Weston with the 'up' "Devonian".

26th May 1958

'Castle' class, No. 5092 *Tresco Abbey*, takes the line into Locking Road with a Whit-Monday excursion train.

Whit-Monday Activity at Locking Road

A large selection of photographs taken from the overbridge at the east end of the two stations at Weston-super-Mare have been included. It is hoped that these pictures will evoke memories of the variety of motive power to be seen (and taken for granted) at many such locations throughout the 1950s and early '60s. If spending a holiday at Weston, why not visit this same bridge and view the scene today – you will notice quite a difference!

Churchward 2-8-0 No. 4703 pulls out of platform 4 with a train of empty coaching stock.

26th May 1958

A 2-6-2T, No. 6107, removes yet another rake of empty stock – a once-familiar scene at Locking Road during summer Saturdays and busy bank holidays. In the right background, a Stanier "Black Five" waits to work back to Bristol, Barrow Road mpd, for servicing.

No. 5015 *Kingswear Castle*, with an 'up' express, gathers speed past the signal box which controlled the lines serving the two stations at Weston – General and Locking Road; both of which are visible in this fine panoramic view. To the right, an ex-GWR 'Hall' class 4-6-0 waits to run forward clear of the turntable road.

Memories of the 'blood and custard' era – the livery of the early-BR period – are recalled as No. 4083 *Abbotsbury Castle* sets off for Bristol with a London-bound train.

18th May 1959

Regular and Excursion Traffic

An unidentified 'Castle' sets back the stock of the "City of Plymouth Holiday Express" into Locking Road station. The stock would be berthed here awaiting the return working to Plymouth later in the day.

"Still retaining a respectable chimney" was the comment written by Norman Lockett in his notebook! No. 7029 *Clun Castle*, not yet fitted with a double chimney, sets off from Weston with the 8am Plymouth to Liverpool train.

18th May 1959

The "West Countryman", an enthusiasts' special arranged by the Locomotive Club of Great Britain, was hauled by ex-LNER A4 class Pacific No. 60022 *Mallard*, working from Waterloo to Exeter and return.

24th February 1963

Locomotive Variety at Tiverton Junction

A bird's-eye view of 0-4-2T No. 1450, shunting the milk tanks brought from the dairy at Hemyock. The main line to Exeter can be seen in the background, and to the right of the signal box, the branch line to Tiverton curves away sharply.

24th February 1963

Nothing in this picture suggests that the Great Western Railway had ceased to exist for nine months! No. 5969 *Honington Hall* runs towards the West Country with the 10.35am Wolverhampton to Penzance express.

4th October 1948

Brent Knoll and Highbridge

Two years later, sister engine No. 5919 *Worsley Hall* carries a BR Western Region smokebox number plate, although careful study will reveal that the heavy freight train includes open wagons still in 'Private ownership' liveries. No. 5919 is seen near Highbridge.

12th October 1950

Cogload

At Cogload, east of Taunton, the original line to the West is joined by the 'direct route', completed between Castle Cary and Cogload in 1906 to permit direct running from Paddington via Westbury, with a saving of some 20 miles between London and the West of England.

The 'down' "Cornish Riviera" draws near to Cogload, hauled by No. 6023 *King Edward II*.

10th October 1953

Taunton

Norman Lockett's only photograph taken at Taunton depicts 'Star' class No. 4022, originally named *King William* but seen here as *Belgian Monarch,* a name which in turn was destined to be removed in May 1940. No. 4022 is about to leave with the 11.20am stopping train to Bristol.

21st June 1937

In charge of a Minehead to Taunton goods train, Collett 0-6-0 No. 2251 drifts along the branch line between Bishops Lydeard and the junction with the main line at Norton Fitzwarren.

3rd May 1934

Pre-War Interlude near Norton Fitzwarren

A GWR 4575 class 2-6-2T sets off along the branch with an afternoon train to Minehead. Now the home of the popular West Somerset Railway, this very picturesque branch line echoes once more to the sounds of Great Western (and S&D!) motive power. Long may it continue to thrive.

3rd May 1934

The 3pm local from Taunton to Exeter includes an elderly clerestory carriage and a once-familiar gas tank wagon. The motive power is provided by 'Saint' class No. 2987 *Bride of Lammermoor.*

17th May 1934

Near Wellington

Back on the main line where, beyond Norton Fitzwarren, westbound trains faced a climb of nearly nine miles, culminating beyond Wellington, in some $2\frac{1}{2}$ miles at 1 in 90:86:80 to the mouth of Whiteball Tunnel.

Ex-LMS 8F class 2-8-0 No. 48420 toils up Wellington Bank with a westbound freight. Most unusually, Norman Lockett failed to record exact details for this and the following photograph, both taken on the same day in October 1957.

'Modified Hall' No. 7916 *Mobberley Hall* climbs towards Whiteball Tunnel with the 'down' "Cornishman".

Wellington Bank

'Castle' class, No. 5086 *Viscount Horne,* attacks the 1 in 80 gradient with the 3.45pm Bristol to Penzance. The location is about a mile short of the entrance to Whiteball Tunnel; the "172½" mile post shows the distance from Paddington as measured by the original route via Bath and Bristol.

10th July 1946

Complete with commemorative bell, the Great Western's most famous locomotive, No. 6000 *King George V,* climbs the bank with the 'down' "Torbay Limited".

21st June 1937

Locomotive Variety on Wellington Bank

Following the nationalisation of Britain's railways in 1948, a most fascinating event for all enthusiasts was the locomotive "exchanges"; the series of trials undertaken on the instruction of the new Railway Executive to establish the strengths and weaknesses of motive power drawn from the designs of the pre-Nationalised companies.

Eleven years after photographing No. 6000 on Wellington Bank, Norman Lockett returned to the Blackdown Hills to capture the exciting spectacle of "foreign" motive power working hard on the gradients leading up to Whiteball Tunnel.

Right, top: Ex-LMS 'Princess Coronation' class 4-6-2, No. 46236 *City of Bradford,* attacks the 1 in 80 section of the climb towards Whiteball, with the 1.30pm Paddington to Penzance.

12th May 1948

Right, below: Two weeks earlier, and on a very wet afternoon, it had been the turn of ex-LNER A4 Pacific, No. 60033 *Seagull* to work the 1.30pm service from Paddington.

28th April 1948

No. 6827 *Llanfrechfa Grange* emerges from the western end of Whiteball Tunnel with a Sunday through train from Wolverhampton to Penzance. The siding seen on the right was used as a refuge for banking engines, after assisting heavy trains from Wellington to the summit. A similar, but much shorter siding, was provided on the 'up' side of the line.

28th August 1955

No. 6012 *King Edward VI,* in charge of the 1.30pm (Sundays) Paddington to Plymouth express, commences the long descent towards Exeter. On the right can be seen the original Whiteball Siding signal box, which was destined soon to be severely damaged by fire, and rebuilt to the less pleasing style seen in the following two pictures.

28th August 1955

Whiteball

The summit of the climb from Norton Fitzwarren comes at the west end of the 1,092 yard long Whiteball Tunnel. Beyond the tunnel, on the 'down' side of the line, stood Whiteball Siding signal box.

Norman Lockett noted the "Cornish Riviera" passing Whiteball at 2.05pm; nearly an hour behind schedule! Perhaps this explains the appearance of No. 4932 *Hatherton Hall,* then allocated to Taunton mpd, which appears to be 'deputising' for the booked engine – more usually a 'King'.

2nd April 1956

Some 25 minutes later, at 2.30pm, more appropriate motive power in the shape of No. 4082 *Windsor Castle,* sweeps past the replacement signal box, on schedule with the 'down' "Torbay Express".

2nd April 1956

Near Burlescombe

From Whiteball summit, the line descends from the Blackdown Hills towards Tiverton Junction, passing through Burlescombe and Sampford Peverell.

(Tiverton Junction and the picturesque branch line to Hemyock are featured in colour on pages 48, 66 and 67.)

No. 3864, a Class 2884 2-8-0, plods up the long climb, near Burlescombe, with a train of coal empties.

22nd April 1957

No. 1015 *County of Gloucester* must be burning coal of somewhat dubious quality as she darkens the sky with the 11.35am (Sundays) Paignton–Paddington express. Both pictures also feature the 'down' goods refuge, which extended between Whiteball and Burlescombe.

29th August 1948

Cowley Bridge Junction

At Cowley Bridge, on the approach to Exeter, the Great Western main line was joined by the ex-Southern Railway route; the "Withered Arm" to Plymouth, north Cornwall and the 'Atlantic Coast'. The Southern Railway held 'running rights' over the two miles of GWR line to Exeter St Davids, before climbing to the SR's own station at Exeter Central, and the main line to Waterloo. (Southern steam on this route to the West will feature in Volume 2 of *The Norman Lockett Collection*.)

No. 4077 *Chepstow Castle* drifts over Cowley Bridge Junction with the 'down' "Royal Duchy", the 1.30pm service from Paddington to Penzance. The rolling stock is in the old GWR chocolate and cream livery, reintroduced by BR on certain WR express services at the commencement of the summer timetable in June 1956.

13th October 1957

Exeter St Davids

No. 5008 *Raglan Castle* rolls into Exeter St Davids with the 'down' "Torbay Express". This was one of the first of the named trains to receive the chocolate and cream livery, reintroduced in June 1956.

9th February 1958

Dawlish Warren

Having run alongside the Exe Estuary, Mogul No. 5364 passes Dawlish Warren and heads towards Dawlish with a freight train bound for Hackney Yard, Newton Abbot.

21st August 1949

Dawlish

After calling at Dawlish, 'Castle' class No. 5057 *Earl Waldegrave* regains speed along the sea wall with the 9.20am local from Kingswear to Exeter St Davids.
16th April 1957

Heading a relief to the 'up' "Devonian", No. 6915 *Mursley Hall* pulls out of Dawlish. The fireman has come across to the driver's side of the cab to enjoy the view. Soon, no doubt, he will be working somewhat harder!
28th September 1957

The Five Tunnels

Any enthusiast interested in the GWR main line in South Devon was almost honour bound to learn by heart the order and lengths of the five tunnels between Dawlish and Teignmouth; Kennaway (209 yards), Coryton (231), Phillot (55), Clerk's (66) and last, and longest, Parson's (512).

An immaculate 'County', No. 1016 *County of Hants,* heads a very mixed assortment of coaching stock past Coryton Cove with the 8am Plymouth to Liverpool express.
16th April 1957

Emerging from the western end of Parson's Tunnel, an unidentified 'King' class locomotive makes a fine sight with the 'down' "Cornish Riviera Express"; the sunlight reflecting off an immaculate engine heading a train in chocolate and cream livery.
28th September 1957

The Sea Wall 1

In ex-works condition, 'West Country' class Pacific No. 34024 *Tamar Valley* commences the run along the sea wall from Parson's Tunnel to Teignmouth, with the 11.25am Exeter to Plymouth local. The use of Southern locomotives on the ex-GWR main line was a regular event to enable SR enginemen to maintain route knowledge should their own route, via Okehampton be closed. Reciprocal workings were run by ex-GWR locomotives and enginemen over the Southern line between Exeter and Plymouth.

20th April 1957

No. 5025 *Chirk Castle,* with the 7.40am Penzance to Paddington express, sweeps round the curve on the approach to Parson's Tunnel, and passes the signal box (the roof of which can be seen) that opened only on summer Saturdays to break the very busy section of line between Dawlish and Teignmouth.

13th April 1954

The Sea Wall 2

Without doubt, the best-known, and possibly the all-time favourite length of Great Western metals; the mile-long section alongside the sea wall between Parson's Tunnel and the East Cliff at Teignmouth. As a personal favourite, I make no apologies for including what is, perhaps, more than 'a fair share' of the very many of Norman Lockett's superb photographs taken on this section of line. (A few more have been included in the accompanying colour section!)

Dwarfed by the towering red sandstone cliffs, BR Standard Pacific, No. 70022 *Tornado* runs along the eastern end of the sea wall, between Sprey Point and Parson's Tunnel, with the 'up' "Devonian".

14th April 1954

An unidentified 2-6-2 Prairie tank leaves Parson's Tunnel with a three-coach local from Exeter to Kingswear.
27th June 1958

Prairies Near Parson's Tunnel

No. 4117 runs along the sea wall towards Parson's Tunnel with another local service, bound for Exeter.
27th June 1958

0-4-2T No. 1450 returns along the picturesque Hemyock branch towards Tiverton, with an enthusiasts' special.
24th February 1963

The Hemyock Branch

An idyllic setting: No. 1450 pauses opposite the Culm Valley Inn at Culmstock. The bonnet of Ivo Peters' Bentley can be seen in the pub car park!

24th February 1963

No. 1450 draws out loaded milk tankers from the dairy at Hemyock – the terminus of the $7\frac{1}{4}$ miles branch line from Tiverton Junction.

24th February 1963

No. 1450 arrives back at Tiverton Junction with a short train of milk tankers and two brake vans, the latter having been used to convey enthusiasts for a trip along this delightful branch line.

24th February 1963

Having called at Teignmouth, No. 4037 *The South Wales Borderers* hurries the 'up' "Devonian" along the sea wall between Sprey Point and Parson's Tunnel. If running to schedule, the time would be about 10.03am, and although the date is late June, the sea wall is all but deserted. Perhaps summer was yet to arrive at this delightful South Devon resort.

27th June 1958

Exeter St Davids Motive Power Depot

Two views of the ex-GWR motive power depot, opposite St Davids station, both taken on 28th September 1962. The top picture includes 'County' class 4-6-0 No. 1023 *County of Oxford*.

"The Royal Duchy" at Newton Abbot

The 'down' "Royal Duchy", the 1.30pm Paddington to Penzance service, calls at Newton Abbot behind No. 7036 *Taunton Castle*.

23rd June 1958

A decade has passed since Nationalisation, yet the illusion of the Great Western Railway lives on. The 'up' "Mayflower", with a 'King' in charge of a train of chocolate and cream liveried stock, spoilt only by the inclusion of a 'blood and custard' restaurant car.

The Great Western Lives On!

Another memory of the "good old days" as a 'Castle' with the "Torbay Express" approaches Shaldon Bridge, Teignmouth.

27th June 1958

With the 'down' line under temporary occupation for engineering works, 'Austerity' 2-8-0 No. 90658 (formerly No. 78717) pilots an unidentified 'Grange' class 4-6-0 'wrong line', with a short vacuum-fitted freight.

21st August 1949

Sunday Afternoon on the Sea Wall

Later in the afternoon, with the engineers' occupation removed, normal running is resumed. No. 6927 *Lilford Hall* runs towards Sprey Point with an Exeter to Kingswear stopping train.

21st August 1949

Teignmouth

Looking absolutely magnificent, No. 7029 *Clun Castle* heads a London-bound train along a deserted sea wall. At first sight, the background scene, which includes the well-known rock promontory – 'The Ness' – appears little different from that seen today. Careful study, however, reveals many changes, not least the development of Shaldon, whilst those buildings on the seaward end of Teignmouth pier have long-since disappeared!

14th April 1954

Passing Teignmouth's 'down outer home' signal, 'Castle' class No. 5058 *Earl of Clancarty* heads away from Teignmouth with a Plymouth–Cardiff excursion. On such a sunny June day, the passengers might have been better enjoying the pleasures of Teignmouth beach!

26th June 1955

Still, possibly, the most photographed railway location in the West Country, where the line emerges through the East Cliff cutting and onto the sea wall. No. 6816 *Frankton Grange* pulls away from Teignmouth station with a Kingswear to Exeter train. The tower of St Michael's church stands prominent in the left background, whilst it is only in recent years that those iron railings guarding the sea wall have been removed, and in fact, some of the posts still survive.

13th April 1954

No. 6024 *King Edward I* approaches Teignmouth station with the 'up' "Cornish Riviera". Teignmouth signal box survived until recent years, and long after the demise of steam I was able to enjoy holiday evening visits to the box which, on summer Saturdays, still remained busy. Note the position of the 'down starting' signal (with the 'inner distant' for Teignmouth Quay below), and the white-painted board provided to aid sighting by locomen.

22nd June 1958

'Castle' class No. 4037 *The South Wales Borderers,* pilots an unidentified sister engine, with an eastbound express alongside the Teign Estuary, on the approach to 'Polly Steps' and Teignmouth Docks. The rear carriage of the train is just emerging from Shaldon Bridge.

Autumn 1957

Shaldon Bridge

West of Teignmouth station, the railway snakes through a deep, stone-walled, cutting emerging to pass the docks which, for more than a century, were served by the railway. Beyond the docks, the line gains the northern bank of the River Teign, which is followed almost as far as Newton Abbot station. A most beautiful stretch of railway, and amongst the most popular of lineside locations are the approaches to Shaldon Bridge, on the outskirts of Teignmouth.

Passing under Shaldon Bridge, No. 7812 *Erlestoke Manor* – then allocated to Newton Abbot mpd (83A) – heads away from Teignmouth with the 1.25pm (Sundays) Exeter to Kingswear local. More than 30 years later, No. 7812 can still be seen running alongside a famous river; this time the Severn. The locomotive, having been superbly restored, now operates on the Severn Valley Railway.

26th August 1956

The 'up' "Torbay Express" left Kingswear at 11.25am, calling at Churston, Paignton, Torquay and Exeter, before running non-stop to Paddington. At weekends, however, the Exeter stop was omitted. With the time recorded by Norman Lockett as 12.25pm, 'Castle' class No. 5078 *Beaufort* (then a favourite choice of engine for this working) is running to schedule, as the train skirts the Teign Estuary on the approach to Shaldon Bridge.

14th April 1954

4500 class 2-6-2T No. 4537 approaches Aller Junction with a Newton Abbot to Kingswear local, comprised of clerestory stock.

31st July 1934

Aller Junction in the 1930s

Rather surprisingly, Norman Lockett took only one photograph (included in the colour section) at the important railway town of Newton Abbot, preferring instead to visit Aller Junction, to the south west of the town. Here was the junction for the lines to Plymouth and to Torbay, the former curving away to commence the ascent of the infamous Dainton Bank.

One of Churchward's powerful 3150 class 2-6-2Ts, No. 3186, heads a Kingswear train away from Aller Junction.

17th May 1936

Attached at Newton Abbot, to assist over the south Devon banks, 'Bulldog' 4-4-0 No. 3336 *Titan* pilots No. 6011 *King James I* with the 5.30am Paddington to Penzance on the approach to Aller Junction.

31st July 1934

No. 4986 *Aston Hall* passes a small orchard between Aller Junction and Kingskerswell, with a Torbay train.

31st July 1934

The Torbay Line

The GWR was, perhaps, the most important factor in the growth of popularity of Torbay. Even as late as 1956, the volume of holiday traffic carried by rail necessitated long-overdue improvement works to increase the capacity of carriage sidings, as well as the provision of a locomotive turntable between Paignton and Goodrington. Now, of course, the most scenic part of the line, the final 6¾ miles from Paignton to Kingswear, is operated by the popular Paignton & Dartmouth Steam Railway.

The "Torbay Express" is again hauled by No. 5078 *Beaufort,* seen here approaching Kingskerswell which, until closure in October 1964, was the first station beyond Newton Abbot on the line to Kingswear.

26th June 1958

'Modified Hall', No. 6965 *Thirlestaine Hall,* climbs the bank from Goodrington, past Waterside, with the 12.34pm service from Bristol. This train was made up of through carriages from Wolverhampton, including a restaurant car, to which were added, at Bristol, carriages off the 9.15am Paddington–Bristol.

24th June 1958

Climbing Towards Churston

Class 5101 2-6-2T No. 4117, climbs towards Churston with the 1.30pm Newton Abbot to Kingswear.

24th June 1958

A "North to West" express of some 50 years ago, commences the hard climb away from Aller Junction with 'Bulldog' 4-4-0 No. 3449 *Nightingale,* assisting No. 4074 *Caldicot Castle.*

18th May 1937

The Ascent of Dainton Bank

No. 4088 *Dartmouth Castle* was recorded at the same location with the 6.05pm Newton Abbot to Plymouth stopping train. The Torbay line may just be discerned in the right background (level with the running plate of the locomotive).

18th May 1937

No. 5017 *St Donats Castle* and No. 4940 *Ludford Hall* lift the 10.30am (Sundays) Paddington to Penzance up the bank towards Stoneycombe. Note the hayrick to the right which has been sheeted over; perhaps to avoid the more traditional protection, a coat of thatch.   17th May 1936

With a lighter load, which included one of the 'super saloons' built by the GWR in 1931 for the boat special trains run from Plymouth Docks to Paddington, 'Star' class No. 4035 *Queen Charlotte* nears Stoneycombe with a westbound express.   17th May 1936

Totnes

Lying at the foot of the dip between Dainton and Rattery Banks, Totnes was the haunt of a stud of banker engines, used to assist both west and eastbound freight traffic. The station was also the junction for the delightful branch line to Ashburton, a section of which, of course, now forms the Dart Valley Railway.

On a sunny pre-war summer evening, and carrying a target identification board (No. 3), 2-6-2T No. 3152 pauses at the 'down' platform at Totnes, between banking duties.

10th July 1934

No. 5016 *Montgomery Castle* restarts the 5.15pm Exeter to Plymouth train from Totnes, and commences the ascent of Rattery Bank. When photographed here by Norman Lockett, *Montgomery Castle* was less than two years old. The coaches were of a somewhat older vintage!

5th June 1934

Running at speed, 'Star' class No. 4026 *Japanese Monarch* (a name destined to be removed by the GWR in January 1941), heads away from Totnes with the 1.30pm Paddington to Penzance express.

5th June 1934

Totnes to Marley Tunnel

Although the glass plate negative has suffered from the ravages of time, this picture represents Norman Lockett's only visit to the lineside at Marley. No. 5011 *Tintagel Castle* climbs the last few yards towards the tunnel mouth with a Paddington to Penzance train.

10th April 1936

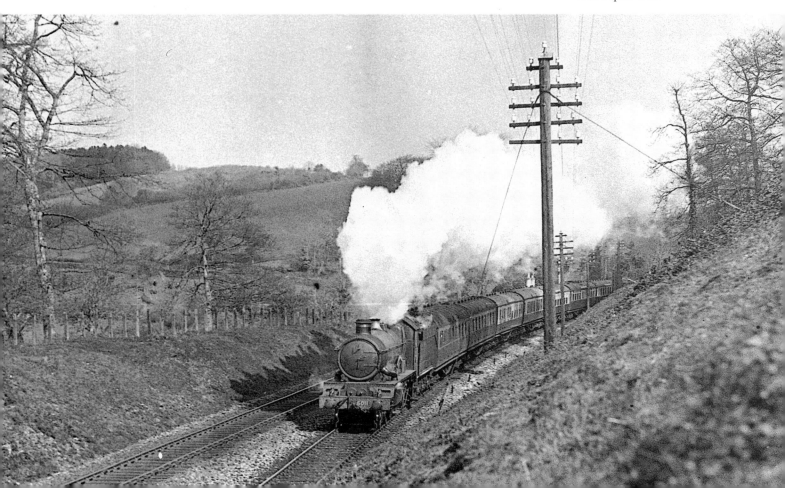

No. 5035 *Coity Castle,* speeds westwards near Ivybridge with a Wolverhampton to Penzance express.

13th April 1938

Ivybridge and Cornwood

No. 4028 *Roumanian Monarch* nears Cornwood with the 4.20pm Newton Abbot to Plymouth. Entering service in 1909 as *King John,* No. 4028 was one of a number of the 'Star' class locomotives bearing the names of British monarchs, and destined to be renamed in 1927 following the introduction of the 'King' class locomotives. Most of the substitute names were, in turn, removed during the progress of the Second World War. No. 4028 became 'nameless' in November 1940.

29th April 1936

No. 5013 *Abergavenny Castle,* seen here less than two years after entering service, in charge of the 'down' "Cornishman" near Cornwood.

1st May 1934

Climbing east of Cornwood, No. 5918 *Walton Hall* assists No. 6009 *King Charles II* with the 1.55pm (Sundays) Plymouth to Paddington.

21st August 1938

Golden Years of the Great Western

The extremes of motive power portrayed in this photograph encapsulate a period of time of great progress by the GWR. No. 3393, built at the turn of the century, is seen passing milepost "236½". This, the distance from Paddington by the original route via Bath and Bristol, led detractors of the GWR to interpret the Company's initials as meaning the "Great Way Round"! Within a few years of No. 3393 entering service however, the GWR would complete its 'direct route' to the West Country, and for a period of more than 25 years, lead the way in all but every facet of railway operation. Not least, in the development of a superb fleet of express passenger locomotives; the 'Saints', 'Stars' and 'Castles', culminating in 1927 with the introduction of the famous 'King' class.

As David Lockett recalls in his introduction to this book, some of his father's earliest photographic 'expeditions' were to the lineside at Hemerdon and here, near Cornwood. This fine study shows 'Bulldog' 4-4-0, No. 3393 *Australia,* assisting No. 6013 *King Henry VIII,* with the 1.55pm (Sundays) Plymouth to Paddington express.

21st August 1938

Another 'Bulldog'/'King' combination is featured as No. 3401 *Vancouver* (built in 1901) assists No. 6022 *King Edward III* (built 1930) with the 12.30pm (Sundays) Penzance to Paddington express.

13th August 1939

Blackford Viaduct

Requiring no assistance, No. 6010 *King Charles I,* sweeps across the graceful Blackford Viaduct, east of Cornwood, with another Sunday Penzance to Paddington express.

13th August 1939

Hemerdon Bank

The major part of Hemerdon Bank consists of two miles of climbing at an uncompromising gradient of 1 in 42. This lifts the GWR line from the estuary of the River Plym at Plympton, on the outskirts of Plymouth, to the foothills of Dartmoor. A severe test of enginemanship, Hemerdon Bank was a wonderful location for watching Great Western motive power being extended to the full.

What can one say? You can almost hear the efforts of No. 6010 *King Charles I* lifting a Plymouth to Paddington express up the bank!

With another impressive effect – (including some steam escaping from where it shouldn't!) No. 2834 labours up the bank with an eastbound freight. Providing essential rear-end assistance, a 2-6-2T is obliterated from view by the exhaust of No. 2834.
26th March 1937

'Bulldog' 4-4-0, No. 3446 *Goldfinch*, and 'King' 4-6-0 No. 6001 *King Edward VII* forge up the bank in fine style with a London-bound express.

13th August 1939

No. 6023 *King Edward II* has a load which presents little difficulty, although it is believed that the leading vehicle may be one of the special GWR bullion vans.

26th March 1937

Hemerdon Bank

No. 5016 *Montgomery Castle* makes light work of the bank with a five-coach local; the 11.10am (Sundays) Plymouth to Newton Abbot.

11th October 1936

On a dull afternoon, considerably greater effort is required from No. 6002 *King William IV* to lift the heavy "North Mail" towards the summit at Hemerdon.

6th May 1936

Kings – Elegant and Otherwise!

In its centenary year (1935), the GWR constructed two special sets of coaches for the "Cornish Riviera Express", which was renamed the "Cornish Riviera Limited". With the 'Centenary Stock' in tow, No. 6002 *King William IV* presents a fine sight on the approach to the summit at Hemerdon with the 'up' 'Limited'.

29th March 1937

In contrast, No. 6014 *King Henry VII*, appears to be making every effort to hide the hideous "streamlining" applied by the GWR in 1935 (a feature of which more later). The train depicted is the 10.30am (Sundays) Plymouth to Paddington.

17th July 1938

In a setting very different from today, 2-6-2T No. 5531 rounds the curve near Marsh Mills, for a run along the picturesque Launceston branch, with the 6.10pm from Plymouth.

19th August 1936

Branch Lines to Launceston and Princetown

A brief departure from the main line, to follow the Launceston branch as far as Clearbrook, and a glimpse of the line from Yelverton to Princetown.

In the early evening, 2-6-2T No. 4591 threads the woods near Clearbrook with the 5.25pm Plymouth Mill-bay–Tavistock service.

21st June 1938

No. 4502 emerges from a delightful setting, as she slows to call at Clearbrook Halt with the 4.30pm Plymouth Millbay to Yelverton train, composed entirely of elderly clerestory stock.

21st June 1938

Norman Lockett's only photograph taken on the $10\frac{1}{2}$ mile branch line from Yelverton to Princetown. With a single clerestory brake in tow, 2-6-2T No. 4402 climbs near Burrator with the 6.55pm Yelverton–Princetown.

20th June 1934

Resting around the turntable inside Laira mpd, this array of tank engines includes a class 1361 0-6-0ST, especially designed for shunting the docks at Plymouth. Alongside this is a 4400 2-6-2T and two variants of the ubiquitous 0-6-0 pannier tank, many of which were used in the Plymouth area, including on the once-intensive 'railmotor' services to and from Saltash.

5th May 1935

Line-ups at Laira

Lined up outside the running shed, a brace of 'Bulldog' 4-4-0s; nameless No. 3431 and sister engine, No. 3401 *Vancouver,* which was based at Laira for many years.

5th May 1935

One minute out from North Road and getting into their stride; 'Bulldog' No. 3342 *Bonaventura* and No. 6015 *King Richard III* accelerate the "Cornish Riviera Express" through Mutley station.

10th July 1934

Plymouth Mutley

Almost within sight of North Road station, Mutley, one of Plymouth's once-numerous suburban stations, was situated immediately to the west of the tunnel which carries the main line under Mutley Plain. An early victim of the competition from road transport, this once-busy station closed to traffic from 2nd March 1939, just eleven months after Norman Lockett took the second of these two photographs.

No. 6018 *King Henry VI* makes an imposing sight with the 10.30am (Sundays) Plymouth–Paddington express. I have to admit though, that my eye was drawn to this photograph by those magnificent gas lamps, behind the second of which can be just seen some of the very tall signals protecting entry to North Road station.

3rd April 1938

The 10.35am (Sundays) Plymouth Mill-bay–Tavistock railmotor pauses at Mutley for custom. Today, the railway here is 'underground', covered by the concrete deck of a car park, but the old Eye Infirmary, prominent in the mid-background, still survives.

3rd April 1938

The Streamline Experiment

In 1935, to celebrate the centenary of the GWR, two locomotives were partially 'streamlined' by the addition of various metal fairings. The result, which appeared to be less than a whole-hearted attempt, came to be regarded as somewhat of a joke. Very soon, some of the streamlining was removed, and one by one the remaining fairings were taken off the locomotives, leaving only the modifications to the cab-front.

Although the glass negatives have suffered deterioration, these views taken at North Road, are thought worthy of inclusion.

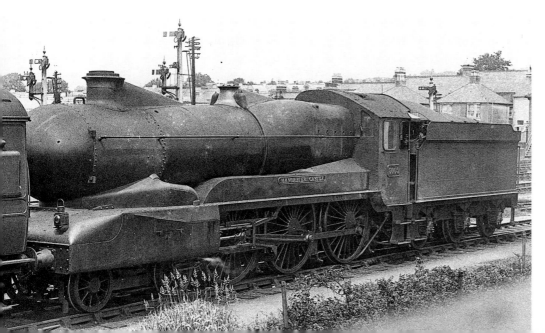

No. 6014 *King Henry VII* and No. 5005 *Manorbier Castle* were photographed in May/June 1935, during the short period when both locomotives retained the full extent of 'streamlining'. The fairings around the cylinders were said to cause overheating, and were the first to be removed. The 'bullet-nose' lasted somewhat longer.

The old North Road station was, perhaps, not one of the GWR's most imposing structures. Obviously, it held no appeal to Norman Lockett, who appears to have ignored the station as a venue for photography, other than the pictures featured here, including this fine portrait of 'Bulldog' No. 3401 *Vancouver*.

5th June 1934

Plymouth: North Road and Millbay

Another of Plymouth's former railway stations, Millbay, was closed to passengers in late-April 1941 when it suddenly became necessary to use the facilities for goods traffic. This followed the destruction of the adjoining goods station during one of the many German air raids on the city.

Seen here, a once-familiar sight from the pre-war era, as 2-6-2T No. 4548 waits to leave with the 5.25pm service to Tavistock.

26th June 1935

No. 5978 *Bodinnick Hall* crosses the bridge with the 'up' "Cornish Riviera". This view, taken from Normandy Way, shows to advantage the two main spans, both 455ft long and providing a headroom of 100ft above high water level.

16th April 1954

The Royal Albert Bridge

Designed by Isambard Kingdom Brunel and opened to public traffic on 4th May 1859, the Royal Albert Bridge carries the railway high above the River Tamar and into Cornwall. Today, it is of course overshadowed by the adjacent Tamar road bridge.

'Britannia' Pacific No. 70024 *Vulcan* slows the 8.45am (Sundays) Penzance to Paddington train, to enable the single-line token to be given up at Royal Albert Bridge signal box.

16th April 1954

No. 6912 *Helmster Hall* regains double track
with the 12 noon Penzance to Paddington
train. The signalman watches from his box,
awaiting receipt of the single line token,
which will be set down by the fireman onto
the arm projecting from the near corner of
the signal box.

16th April 1954

A pre-war view of the bridge, seen from the
Cornish side at Saltash station and showing a hillside which today is covered by the
western development of Plymouth. The
bridge portals display the legend "I. K.
Brunel Engineer 1859".

September 1934

No. 4929 *Goytrey Hall* heads westwards near St Germans with a Wolverhampton–Penzance express.

1st August 1936

Early Evening Near St Germans

No. 4932 *Hatherton Hall* lifts the 5.15pm stopping train from Plymouth to Truro up a steep gradient near St Germans. The tree on the right leaves no doubt as to the direction of the prevailing winds on this exposed section of line!

1st August 1939

Bodmin Road

A print taken from a plate which, sadly, has been damaged – but it is still a nice study of No. 2839 with inside steampipes and the original square front drop-end to the running plate. No. 2839, with a westbound class D freight, had paused at Bodmin Road to take on water.

15th August 1934

Near Trerule

The once-familiar Great Western scene of an 0-6-0PT sandwiched between two pairs of railmotor coaches. Seen here is an evening train from Plymouth Millbay to Liskeard, close to the junction proposed by the GWR for a new railway to Looe. This scheme was abandoned as a result of the war and never brought to fruition.

15th August 1939

A Last Pre-War Lineside Visit

These photographs, the very last by Norman Lockett in the pre-war era, were taken just 19 days before Britain declared war on 3rd September 1939. In reality, they represent the final days of the 'real' Great Western, for the old Company was never to regain such heights in the few post-war years before Nationalisation of Britain's railways.

Above: Crewe to Penzance train, hauled by No. 4953 *Pitchford Hall,* approaches Trerule box. No. 4953 is now undergoing restoration to working order at the Dean Forest Railway.

15th August 1939

Right: Little more than a year old, No. 5071 *Clifford Castle* hurries up the long climb from St Germans, passing near to Trerule Foot with the 1.40pm Paddington to Penzance. No. 5071 was destined, in September 1940, to be renamed *Spitfire* in honour of the Battle of Britain aircraft. The war was to result in Norman Lockett moving away from Plymouth, and he never progressed any further west than Trerule in pursuit of railway photography.

15th August 1939

A sight to gladden the hearts of steam enthusiasts! No. 7808 *Cookham Manor*, looking somewhat "down at heal", is still able to come to the assistance of a diesel-hydraulic 'Hymek' with a Bristol-bound parcels train. No. 7808 was destined to be purchased by the Great Western Society, and today resides at their magnificent headquarters at Didcot.

Bath Spa

On a lovely sunny evening, a 'Castle' brings the 5.05pm Paddington to Weston-super-Mare into Bath Spa.

Nearing Bathampton

An eastbound train heads up the main line towards Bathampton, passing the remains of the old Bathampton West signal box.

Box Middle Hill

BR Class 3 2-6-2T No. 82036 emerges from Middle Hill Tunnel, to the east of Box station, with the 1.10pm (SO) Calne to Weston-super-Mare.

Limpley Stoke Valley

0-4-2T No. 1444 nears Claverton between Limpley Stoke and Bathampton, with a special train run by the Great Western Society.

Hawkeridge Junction

No. 6851 *Hurst Grange* passes Hawkeridge Junction with the 11.10am (SO) Wolverhampton – Weymouth through train. The line curving away to the right is the Westbury East Chord.

An ex-GWR 'Hall', running into Westbury from the Trowbridge direction, with the 12.50pm Cardiff to Brighton. Behind the leading coach, an 0-6-0PT acting as station pilot, waits on the Patney line, built by the GWR and opened in 1900 as part of the direct route from Paddington to the West of England, the last section of which was completed in 1906.

11th March 1963

Westbury

Ex-LMS Ivatt Class 4MT 2-6-0 No. 43115, runs past Westbury North box, whilst a BR Class 5 waits at platform 4 with a local service to Bristol. The North signal box, together with the impressive array of semaphore signals, survived until May 1984, when they were demolished as part of the West of England resignalling programme.

10th October 1964

An 0-6-0PT, with a train of empties for Whatley Quarry, heads away from Frome towards the exchange sidings at Hapsford.

Whatley Quarry Stone Trains

Some 2½ miles west of Frome, the now truncated North Somerset branch, which ran from Frome to Bristol, today still serves a large stone quarry at Whatley with the line to Radstock scheduled for re-opening as the Somerset & Avon Railway.

A return working of loaded stone approaches Frome.

Blatchbridge Junction

The Frome avoiding line, constructed by the GWR in 1933, extends from Clink Road Junction in the east, to Blatchbridge Junction in the west, a distance of just over two miles. The 11.10am (SO) Wolverhampton to Weymouth is in the charge of No. 6851 *Hurst Grange* travelling westwards from Blatchbridge.

29th August 1964

Brewham Summit

A 'down' train, hauled by a 'Hall', the number of which is just not discernible, passes Brewham signal box.

Under clear signals, a 'King' climbs Brewham Bank with the 'up' "Royal Duchy" the leading coach of which is a brake composite from the GWR 'Centenary Stock' of 1935.

Brewham Bank

No longer maintained in the pristine condition of the other locomotives seen in earlier Norman Lockett colour photographs, this 'Castle' was noted as making a rapid ascent of Brewham Bank with a London-bound train.

Castle Cary

Not what it might seem! Norman Lockett noted that the Bristol to Weymouth dmu had 'come to the rescue' of No. 6821 *Leaton Grange*, which had failed near Castle Cary. The unusual signal box dates from 1942, the former box having been destroyed by enemy action.

Evershot

In the early 1950s, operating control of the ex-GWR line south of Castle Cary to Yeovil and Weymouth, passed to the Southern Region. Hence the SR livery and upper quadrant signals seen here at Evershot station. No. 6821 *Leaton Grange*, here in working order, passes through the station with a 'perishables' train from Weymouth Quay.

Bristol Temple Meads

After a 13 minute wait at Bristol, 'Castle' class No. 5090 *Neath Abbey* restarts the 8.20am Weston-super-Mare to Paddington from Temple Meads. This service called at Bath before running non-stop to London.
24th April 1959

We return to Bristol Temple Meads, this time to travel east along the original Great Western line, as far as Box. Then, from Bathampton, via the Limpley Stoke Valley to join the old Wilts, Somerset & Weymouth branch. A 20 mile section of this latter line, between Westbury and Castle Cary, was to become, in 1906, part of the new 'direct' route from Paddington to the West Country.

Part 2: Bristol to Bath, Westbury and Castle Cary

As mentioned in the Introduction to Part 1, Temple Meads was a joint station shared by the GWR and the LMS. In addition to through services to the Midlands and the North of England, local LMS services ran between Bristol, Bath and Gloucester. LMS Compound 4-4-0, No. 40917, approaches Temple Meads with a train from Gloucester.
22nd August 1956

Dr Day's Bridge Junction

The Bristol to Bath main line passes from right to left in the background. No. 7018 *Drysllwyn Castle,* has turned north at Bristol Temple Meads East Junction, and crosses over Dr Day's Bridge Junction with the 'up' "Bristolian". The lines to the left lead to North Somerset Junction, and in addition to through trains between South Wales and the South Coast, were used by some North to West services avoiding Temple Meads station.

1st October 1958

St Anne's Park

No. 4080 *Powderham Castle* emerges from Fox's Wood No. 2 Tunnel – sometimes known as St Anne's Tunnel – with the 11am Brighton to Cardiff. This train avoided reversal at Temple Meads, by taking the direct line to Stapleton Road via the spur (seen in the previous photograph) from North Somerset to Dr Day's Bridge Junction.

5th June 1957

An early opportunity is taken to top up the tender of 2-6-0 No. 9319, heading eastwards with the 2.38pm Bristol to Reading train.
6th May 1953

Fox's Wood Water Troughs

The water troughs at Fox's Wood were installed, along with troughs at Goring (Berkshire) in 1895, to enable traffic to run non-stop between Paddington and Exeter and, via the Severn Tunnel, between London and Newport. In later years, when the West of England traffic ran via Westbury, and London to South Wales trains via the Badminton direct line, the troughs at Fox's Wood were used less intensively. In the last years of steam, only through trains between Brighton, Portsmouth and Cardiff regularly used the troughs, which were taken out of use in May 1961, after which locomotives took on water at Bath Spa.

An immaculate No. 5005 *Manorbier Castle* takes on water with the 1pm Cardiff to Brighton. No. 5005 looks somewhat more akin to a GWR 'Castle' than when last seen at Plymouth in 1935!

3rd October 1953

Bath Spa – East End

The eastern approach to Bath Spa is elevated on continuous arches before the line, crossing the River Avon, reaches the station.

No. 5040 *Stokesay Castle* enters the station with a Paddington to Bristol express.
October 1957

Opposite: 'Modified Hall', No. 7901 *Dodington Hall*, crosses the river with the 2.33pm Portsmouth to Bristol Temple Meads. The line in the left foreground served the bay platform which, in latter years, was sometimes used for local services to Chippenham and Swindon.

27th July 1955

Twerton Tunnel

Two miles west of Bath, the GWR line passes through Twerton Tunnel. The portals at both ends of this tunnel are most impressive; the high-arched mouths surmounted by castellated walls and flanked by attractive segmental turrets (the latter complete with 'arrow slits'!).

Previous page: WD 'Austerity' 2-8-0, No. 90069, allocated to 86A Newport, Ebbw Junction mpd, heads towards home with a heavy freight train.

22nd May 1956

Right: This photograph provides a closer view of the attractive portal at the west end of Twerton Tunnel. Mogul No. 6360, emerges into the early evening sunlight with a Bristol-bound parcels train.

11th July 1956

Bath Spa

The "Merchant Venturer" was booked to run the 107 miles from Paddington to Bath non-stop in 1 hr 46 min. 'Castle' class, No. 5087 *Tintern Abbey*, slows for a 'right-time' arrival at Bath.

27th September 1954

No. 6021 *King Richard II* approaches the station with the 4.15pm Paddington–Plymouth.

31st May 1958

Sydney Gardens, Bath

Heading eastwards from Bath Spa, the line passes through Sydney Gardens. Always a popular place for photographing, or just watching the passing trains.

Early spring: with the trees yet to break into leaf, and an audience of only three, No. 1028 *County of Warwick* drifts through the park with the 1.15pm Paddington to Weston-super-Mare, having run non-stop from London.

18th April 1956

Late summer: all eyes turn to watch No. 6915 *Mursley Hall* with the 1.18pm Paddington to Weston-super-Mare; a service which 'those in the know' tended to avoid. Despite leaving the Capital only three minutes after the service featured above, the 1.18pm reached Bath 1 hr 11 min after the 1.15pm!

2nd August 1955

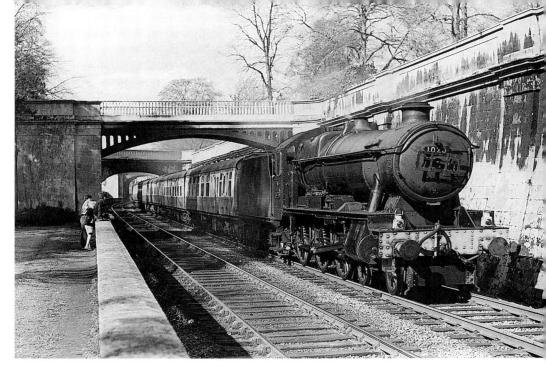

Near Bathampton

Approaching Bathampton, two miles east of Bath, goods loops were provided on both sides of the main running lines. Immediately beyond Bathampton station (now closed), the important cross-country link line branched away towards Westbury and Salisbury.

The north west hillside terraced houses of the City of Bath provide the backdrop, as GWR Mogul, No. 9312, hurries eastwards along the main line towards Bathampton, with an 'up' parcels train.

11th May 1958

No. 6003 *King George IV* speeds past the west end of the 'down' goods loop with the 1.15pm Paddington to Weston-super-Mare.

2nd October 1958

At a date by which only ten of the famous 'Castle' class locomotives remained in service, No. 7029 *Clun Castle* heads a 'farewell tour' towards Bath.

24th January 1965

Box

Some licence has been taken to 'stray' a few miles from the route followed in this part of the book, to enable inclusion of these two photographs taken at Box, on the main line a little to the east of Bathampton.

No. 5030 *Shirburn Castle,* in 'ex-works' condition, positively gleams as she restarts the 5pm Swindon–Bristol train from Box. The western portal of Middle Hill Tunnel can be seen in the background.

25th May 1955

No. 5090 *Neath Abbey* is seen here leaving Middle Hill Tunnel with the 8.20am Weston-super-Mare to Paddington.

18th June 1958

No. 7015 *Carn Brea Castle* begins to regain speed after slowing at Bathampton to take the Bradford line, with the 10.10am (Sundays) Bristol Temple Meads to Weymouth.

4th April 1958

Bathampton – Holmes Siding

From the main line at Bathampton, the Bradford branch turns away southwards on a very sharp curve. After a $\frac{1}{4}$ mile the line passes over an occupation crossing. Here, for many years, there was a siding providing rail access to Messrs Holmes timber yard.

Later, the same morning, BR 'Britannia' No. 70023 *Venus,* passes the access to Holmes Siding with the 9.30am (Sundays) Cardiff to Portsmouth.

4th April 1958

Heading towards Claverton with the 4.32pm Bristol to Weymouth train, No. 5964 *Wolseley Hall* is about a mile out from Bathampton, at a point where the line hugs the river bank.

22nd May 1957

The Limpley Stoke Valley

From Bathampton, the railway follows the River Avon along the very scenic Limpley Stoke valley towards Bradford-on-Avon– a route also followed by the Kennet & Avon Canal, which was reopened throughout in 1990.

Against a wooded backcloth – known locally as "Sally-in-the-Woods" – No. 5962 *Wantage Hall* heads towards Dundas Aqueduct with the 5.03pm Bristol to Weymouth train. (On looking through an old 'loco-spotting book', I noted that *Wantage Hall* was the only member of the '59XX' series that I had failed to see – and here she is, only 20 minutes away from my home town!)

29th July 1953

A spotless Mogul, No. 6320, drifts round the reverse curves near Claverton with a Bristol-bound train. How well the railway fits into the landscape compared with today's motorways!

22nd May 1957

The 4.35pm Cardiff to Portsmouth train, drawn by No. 6967 *Willesley Hall,* runs along the valley towards Limpley Stoke.

21st May 1952

Westbury

Castle' class, No. 5092 *Tresco Abbey,* rolls into Westbury with the 'down' "Royal Duchy". Westbury North signal box controlled the junction of the original line from Trowbridge, seen curving away to the left under the road bridge, and the 'Berks & Hants' line opened by the GWR in 1900 between Westbury and Patney. This was to form part of the new 'direct' route to the West, completed in 1906.

21st August 1957

Frome

The 4.10pm Weymouth Town to Paddington enters Frome station behind No. 5997 *Sparkford Hall* (rather appropriate in view of the address of our publishers!). A connection to Bristol, running via Radstock West and the North Somerset line, was provided at Frome to carry mail brought up from Weymouth and the Channel Islands.

6th August 1957

Upton Scudamore Bank

The line from Westbury to Salisbury was always Great Western property, but following Nationalisation, operating responsibility passed, on 2nd April 1950, to the Southern Region. I couldn't resist, however, including just one of Norman Lockett's photographs taken near Upton Scudamore, on the steep climb from Westbury towards Warminster.

'Britannia' No. 70023 *Venus* makes a vigorous ascent of the bank with the 12.50pm Cardiff to Brighton train, passing Ivo Peters who had accompanied Norman to the lineside.

5th October 1959

Near Witham

GWR pannier tank, No. 8795, scurries down the main line, with the 6pm Frome–Yatton service.

14th April 1962

Brewham Summit

Brewham signal box, west of Bruton, marked the summit of an eight mile climb from Frome, after which (apart from two small 'humps') the line falls for nearly 30 miles to Athelney, on the Somerset Levels. No. 4077 *Chepstow Castle* passes Brewham signal box with the 3.30pm Paddington–Plymouth express.

July 1958

Castle Cary

Following the opening of the final link forming the direct route to the West, Castle Cary became a junction for the new line to Somerton and Taunton, and the original 'Wilts, Somerset & Weymouth' line, which heads southwards towards Yeovil and Dorchester. This latter line came into the operating control of the Southern Region from 1950, and will feature in the next volume of *The Norman Lockett Collection.* No. 7921 *Edstone Hall* runs into Castle Cary from the original 'WS&W' line with a troop train from Weymouth to Penzance.

12th August 1962